M000074643

To Rachel

From ❤ Peggy

Date

THE FRUIT OF THE SPIRIT IS

Peace

HONOR BOOKS

Tulsa, Oklahoma

The Fruit of the Spirit is PEACE
ISBN #1-56292-659-4
Copyright © 2000 by Honor Books
P.O. Box 55388
Tulsa, Oklahoma 74155

Compiled and edited by Paul M. Miller.

Peace I leave with you; my peace I give you. I do not
give to you as the world gives. Do not let your hearts
be troubled and do not be afraid.

—JOHN 14:27

A BUSHEL OF *Peace*

"There's a deep settled peace in my soul," sang the congregation. Out of the corner of my eye, I saw the guy next to me wiping his eyes.

Peace is the universal plea. While the billows of sin and war and madness roll near, the world attempts to legislate or strong-arm peace. But, like the fellow next to me understood, peace on earth begins with the assurance of "a deep settled peace" within individual hearts.

The solution? "You will keep in perfect peace him whose mind is steadfast, because he trusts in you" (Isaiah 26:3).

❧

According to Psalm 1, a true believer is like a fruit tree that is planted by a nourishing stream. Just as peaches are picked from such a tree, the Apostle Paul says that Christian disciples are expected to bear spiritual fruit that is nourished by God's Holy Spirit (Galatians 5:22).

As we were seated after singing that song of peace, the fellow to my right leaned over and whispered behind his hand, "My inner war ceased when I surrendered myself to the Spirit's work. I thank God daily for the fruit of peace."

—PAUL M. MILLER

A SUBLIME PROMISE

The LORD gives strength to his people;
the LORD blesses his people with peace.

—PSALM 29:11

While this poet has world peace in mind, the children of God can interpret this as the cessation of inner war.

FROM *CREATE GREAT PEACE*

Would you end war?

Create great peace. . . .

The peace that demands all of a man,

His love, his life, his veriest self.

—JAMES ROBERT OPPENHEIMER

PEACE

With eager heart and will in fire,
I strove to win my great desire.
"Peace shall be mine," I said; but life
Grew bitter in the barren strife.

Broken at last, I bowed my head,
Forgetting all myself, and said,
"Whatever comes, His will be done";
And in that moment peace was won.

—HENRY VAN DYKE

❧

Seek peace and pursue it.

—PSALM 34:14

NOTHING TO FEAR

Growing up in the San Francisco Bay area, I was privileged to witness wonderful cultural events, but nothing could surpass the opportunity I had with other junior high kids to attend one of the meetings that resulted in the formation of the United Nations.

Representatives from my school were perched up in the second balcony at the War Memorial Opera House. The speaker for that momentous occasion was Eleanor Roosevelt.

I didn't understand a lot of what Mrs. Roosevelt said. Her voice was high-pitched and shaky, and she had a slight accent. But I well remember a reference to her late husband's oft-quoted words, "We have nothing to fear but fear itself."

Today, as I seek for inner peace, those words strike a responsive chord, and I recall this verse, "There is no fear in love. But perfect love drives out fear" (1John 4:18). That is the source of inner peace.

—PAUL M. MILLER

INWARD PEACE

Calm soul of all things! Make it mine
To feel, amid the city's jar,
That there abides a peace of thine,
Man did not make, and cannot mar!

—MATTHEW ARNOLD

I am searching for that which every man seeks—
peace and rest.

—DANTE ALIGHIERE

THERE'S A PEACE IN MY HEART

There's a peace in my heart that the world never gave,

A peace it cannot take away.

Though the trials of life may surround like a cloud,

I've a peace that has come here to stay!

—ANNE S. MURPHY

Rx FOR PEACE OF MIND AND HEART

Order your soul.

Reduce your wants.

Live in charity.

Associate in Christian community.

Obey the laws.

Trust in Providence.

—ST. AUGUSTINE

A REMEDY

When at night you cannot sleep,
talk to the Shepherd and stop counting sheep.

—ANONYMOUS

If there is to be any peace, it will come
through being, not having.

—HENRY MILLER

The meek will inherit the land and enjoy great peace.

—PSALM 37:11

THOU WILT KEEP HIM IN PERFECT PEACE

❧

O He is the only perfect Resting Place!

He giveth perfect peace.

"Thou wilt keep him in perfect peace,

Whose mind is stayed on Thee."

—FLOYD HAWKINS

WAR VS. *Peace*

"Whata'ya reading?"

"*War and Peace.*"

"Really? I'll take the latter."

"What do ya mean 'the latter?' Ya gotta have both."

"Both? All I want is peace. There's been too much war."

"Maybe you can't appreciate peace until you know war."

"Kinda like the old joke, 'I'm hittin' myself on the head with a hammer, 'cause it feels so good when I stop.'"

"No, it's more like the old song, 'There's a deep settled peace in my soul. Tho' the billows of sin near me roll, He abides; Christ abides.'"

—PAUL M. MILLER

A PHYSICIAN ON PEACE

It takes more distress and poison to kill someone
who has peace of mind and loves life.

—BERNIE S. SIEGEL, M.D.

Great peace have they who love your law, and
nothing can make them stumble.

—PSALM 119:165

People should be beautiful in every way—
in their faces, in the way they dress, in their thoughts,
and in their innermost selves there must be peace.

—ANTON CHEKHOV

THREEFOLD NATURE OF PEACE

Peace with God

Peace within ourselves

Peace with other people

—JERRY BRIDGES

If it is possible, as far as it depends on you,

live at peace with everyone.

—ROMANS 12:18

THE ONLY HOPE FOR PEACE

On Good Friday following the assassination of Martin Luther King Jr., I was in Georgetown, Guyana, with a church youth group. After service in the Anglican cathedral, I walked the garden maze in a park across the street.

I sensed someone following me. Nervously, I stopped and faced a tall black man. "What do you want?" I demanded.

"Why did you Americans kill Dr. King? He was the Negro's only hope for peace."

"Sir," I responded, "every person's hope for peace is the Man whose death we remember today, and whose resurrection we celebrate Sunday."

—PAUL M. MILLER

THE PRAYER OF SERENITY

❧

God, give us grace to accept with serenity
the things that cannot be changed,

courage to change the things which
should be changed,

and the wisdom to distinguish the one
from the other.

—REINHOLD NIEBUHR

THE SOURCE OF MY CONTENTMENT

I will sprinkle clean water on you,
and you will be clean. . . .
I will give you a new heart
and put a new spirit in you;
I will remove from you your heart of
stone
and give you a heart of flesh.
And I will put my Spirit in you. . . .
You will be my people,
and I will be your God.

—EZEKIEL 36:25-28

PEACE, PERFECT *Peace*

Peace, perfect peace, in this dark world of sin?

The blood of Jesus whispers peace within.

It is enough; earth's struggles soon shall cease,

And Jesus, call us to heav'n perfect peace.

—EDWARD T. BICKERSTETH

TWAIN ON

From his cradle to his grave a man never does a single thing which has any first and foremost object save one—to secure peace of mind and spiritual comfort for himself.

—MARK TWAIN

COLLECT FOR *Peace*

Most holy God, the source of all good desires, all right judgements, and all just works, give to us, Your servants, that peace which the world cannot give, so that our minds may be fixed on the doing of Your will, and that we, being delivered from fear of all enemies, may live in peace and quietness; through the mercies of Christ Jesus our Savior. Amen.

THE SHEPHERD

For he hears the lamb's innocent call,

And he hears the ewes' tender reply;

He is watchful while they are in peace,

For they know when their shepherd is nigh.

—WILLIAM BLAKE

THE LORD BLESS YOU

The LORD bless you and keep you;
The LORD make his face shine upon
you and be gracious to you;
The LORD turn his face toward you
and give you peace.

—NUMBERS 6:24-26

Only one thing is necessary for peace; to possess God.

—HENRI FREDERICK AMIEL

Fear knocked at the door.

Faith answered.

No one was there.

—OLD ENGLISH LEGEND

THE SHEPHERD OF PEACE

Bethlehem . . . out of you will come for me one who will rule over Israel. . . . He will stand and shepherd his flock in the strength of the LORD, in the majesty of the name of the LORD his God. They will live securely. . . . And he will be their peace.

—MICAH 5:2, 4-5

Lord, make me an instrument of Thy peace;

Where hate rules, let me bring love;

Where malice, forgiveness;

Where disputes, reconciliation;

Where error, truth;

Where despair, hope;

Where darkness, Thy light;

Where sorrow, joy.

—ST. FRANCIS OF ASSISI

In a world filled with causes for worry and anxiety . . . we need the peace of God standing guard over our hearts and minds.

—JERRY W. MCCANT

Blessed are the peacemakers,
for they will be called sons of God.

—MATTHEW 5:9

RECOLLECTIONS FROM 1942

My dad was an air raid warden when I was ten during WWII. We lived in Long Beach, California, where aircraft plants made us an enemy target. One little-known fact is that on a Sunday evening in 1942, a squadron of Japanese reconnaissance planes flew over our city and set off the air raid sirens.

While the warnings whined, our apartment-house neighbors, along with Mom and me, trooped down into the basement. Dad grabbed his civil defense helmet and went into the blacked-out neighborhood.

After a bit we heard the booms of anti-aircraft guns. I snuggled closer to Mom, but after a bit, the firing stopped and the all-clear siren sounded. In a few minutes, Dad came down the steps to where we were hiding. In his hand was a piece of shrapnel that had dented his metal hat.

When my own son was ten, he held that piece of his grandpa's shrapnel and asked me, "How come people don't want to live in peace?"

My answer? "Son, as long as people are at war within themselves, there will be no peace."

—PAUL M. MILLER

Forgiving those who hurt us is a key to personal peace.

—G. WEATHERLEY

LINCOLN'S PEACE OF MIND

I am not bound to win, but I am bound to be true. I am not bound to succeed, but I am bound to live up to what light I have. I must stand with anybody that stands right; stand with him while he is right, and part with him when he goes wrong.

—ABRAHAM LINCOLN

Make every effort to do what leads to peace.

—ROMANS 14:19

THE SIMPLE FAITH

Before me, even as behind,
God is, and all is well.

—JOHN GREENLEAF WHITTIER

STILL, STILL WITH THEE

Still, still with Thee,

When purple morning breaketh,

When the bird waketh,

And the shadows flee;

Fairer than morning,

Lovelier than the daylight,

Dawns the sweet consciousness,

I am with Thee.

—HARRIET BEECHER STOWE

❧

Let the peace of Christ rule in your
hearts, since as members of one body
you were called to peace.

—COLOSSIANS 3:15

*Relate this thought to matters
of the human spirit.*

The mere absence of war is not peace.

—JOHN F. KENNEDY

The prophet is looking toward a new age. He is the same person who foretold the coming of the Prince of Peace.

They will beat their swords into plowshares

and their spears into pruning hooks.

Nation will not take up sword against nation,

nor will they train for war anymore.

—ISAIAH 2:4

Looking for peace is like looking for a turtle
with a mustache: you won't be able to find it.
But when your heart is ready, peace will come
looking for you.

—AJAHN CHAH

REMEMBER THIS SONG?

BOYS: I have the peace that passes
understanding, down in my heart.

GIRLS: Where?

BOYS: Down in my heart!

GIRLS: Where?

BOYS: Down in my heart. I have the peace that
passes understanding, down in my heart.

BOTH: Down in my heart to stay.

Whoever would love life and see good days
. . . must seek peace and pursue it.

—1 PETER 3:10-11

Peace does not rest in charters and covenants alone.
It lies in the hearts and minds of the people.

—JOHN F. KENNEDY

All men desire peace but few indeed desire
those things which make for peace.

—THOMAS Á KEMPIS

When the

Power of Love

Overcomes the

Love of Power,

The World Will

Know Peace.

—ANONYMOUS

ADVICE

Be good, keep your feet dry, your eyes open, your
heart at peace, and your soul in the joy of Christ.

—THOMAS MERTON

HYMN TO CONTENTMENT

Lovely, lasting peace of mind,

Sweet delight of human kind.

—THOMAS PARNELL

Make every effort to live in peace with all men.

—HEBREWS 12:14

I do not want the peace which
passeth understanding.
I want the understanding
that bringeth peace.

—HELEN KELLER

The peace is won by accompanying God into battle.

—EIVIND JOSEF BERGGRAVE

A PRAYER FOR
PEACE ON EARTH

If my people, who are called by my name,

will humble themselves and pray

and seek my face

and turn from their wicked ways,

then will I hear from heaven

and forgive their sin

and will heal their land.

2 CHRONICLES 7:14

IT IS WELL WITH MY SOUL

When peace like a river, attendeth my way,
When sorrows like sea billows roll;
Whatever my lot, Thou hast taught me to say,
"It is well, it is well with my soul."

Tho' Satan should buffet, tho' trials should come,
Let this blest assurance control,
That Christ hath regarded my helpless estate,
And hath shed His Own blood for my soul.

My sin—O the bliss of this glorious tho't—
My sin—not in part, but the whole—
Is nailed to His cross and I bear it no more!
Praise the Lord, praise the Lord, O my soul!

And, Lord haste the day when the faith shall be sight,
The clouds be rolled back as a scroll
The trump shall resound and the Lord shall descend.
Even so—it is well with my soul.

—H. G. SPAFFORD

Near to the heart of God

There is a place of full release,

Near to the heart of God;

A place where all is joy and peace,

Near to the heart of God.

— C. B. MCAFEE

TRANQUILITY AND PEACE

Keep your heart in peace; let nothing in this world disturb it: all things have an end. In all circumstances, however hard they may be, we should rejoice, rather than be cast down, that we may not lose the greatest good, the peace and tranquility of our souls.

—ST. JOHN OF THE CROSS

KEEP THE PEACE

The tall skinny boy had a sweatshirt on that shouted, "Keep the Peace" in what we used to call a psychedelic design. We were standing near a campfire and having a conversation about the war that was tearing him up inside. Glancing down at his shirt, he remarked wistfully, "Keep it? I don't even have it." We prayed together that night. I asked God's Spirit to give him the witness of His presence—a sense of peace and tranquility.

What I prayed for that young man, I have prayed for myself—and I pray for you who read these words.

—PAUL M. MILLER

A PRAYER FOR PEACE

Eternal God, in whose perfect kingdom no sword is drawn but the sword of righteousness, no strength known but the strength of love: So mightily spread abroad Your Spirit, that all peoples may be gathered under the banner of the Prince of Peace, as children of one Father; to whom be dominion and glory, now and forever. Amen.

—THE BOOK OF
COMMON PRAYER

Shakespeare understood that the
person at peace with himself is honest
and straightforward with others
and with himself.

This above all: To thine own self be true;

And it must follow, as the night the day,

Thou canst not then be false to any man.

—WILLIAM SHAKESPEARE,
from *Hamlet*

LIKE A RIVER GLORIOUS

Like a river glorious is God's perfect peace,

Over all victorious in its bright increase.

Perfect, yet it floweth fuller ev'ry day;

Perfect yet it groweth deeper all the way.

—FRANCES R. HAVERGAL

❧

Do not be anxious about anything, but in everything, by prayer and petition, with thanksgiving, present your requests to God. And the peace of God, which transcends all understanding, will guard your hearts and your minds in Christ Jesus.

—PHILIPPIANS 4:6-7

He who dwells in the shelter of the Most
High will rest in the shadow of the Almighty.

—PSALM 91:1

PEACE LIKE A RIVER

Believers who attend recitals performed by operatic diva
Marilyn Horne are often surprised to hear her perform
an old gospel hymn, sung as gently as a lullaby.

> *Shall we gather at the river;*
> *Where bright angel feet have trod,*
> *With its crystal tide forever,*
> *Flowing by the throne of God.*

Then with even greater conviction she continues;

> *Soon we'll reach the shining river,*
> *Soon our pilgrimage will cease;*
> *Soon our happy hearts will quiver*
> *With the melody of peace.*

After a huge ovation, the singer will often explain, "When I sing that lovely old song, I think of my mother who used to sing it while she held me when I was unhappy. Today when my world is awry and I sing about the river, I feel peace come over my spirit."

Yes, we'll gather at the river,
The beautiful, the beautiful river;
Gather with the saints at the river
That flows by the throne of God.

—PAUL M. MILLER

 FACT 1

WE ARE INHERITORS OF PEACE

Since we have been justified through faith, we have
peace with God through our Lord Jesus Christ.

—ROMANS 5:1

Peace FACT 2

CHRIST IS OUR PEACE

For he himself is our peace.

—EPHESIANS 2:14

Peace FACT 3

PEACE IS TO BE CLAIMED

Peace I leave with you; my peace I give you. I do not
give to you as the world gives. Do not let you hearts
be troubled and do not be afraid.

—JOHN 14:27

Peace FACT 4

PEACE INVOLVES RIGHTEOUSNESS

The fruit of righteousness will be peace; the effect of
righteousness will be quietness and confidence forever.

—ISAIAH 32:17

 FACT 5

SPIRIT-CONTROLLED PEACE

The mind of sinful man is death, but the mind
controlled by the Spirit is life and peace.

—ROMANS 8:6

Peace FACT 6

CONTINUOUS PEACE

May the Lord of peace himself give you peace at all times.

—2 THESSALONIANS 3:16

THE REST IN PEACE

Upon God's will I lay me down,

As child upon its mother's breast,

No silken couch, nor softest bed,

Could ever give me such deep rest.

—TERSTEEGEN

SERENITY FROM SECURITY

Our peace is a result of God's making
His peace with us.

—GREG OGDEN

When God signs a peace treaty,
it is signed for perpetuity.

—R. C. SPROUL

SHALOM

The Hebrew word for *peace* is *shalom*. Shalom is not so much the absence of war but the presence of a benevolent, just, and honorable king.

—MEYER K. WINTERBAUM

❦

A heart at peace gives life to the body.

—PROVERBS 14:30

PEACE AT ALL COSTS

The knot of rain-soaked demonstrators huddled together under a grocery store awning caught my eye. Actually, it was the message on one of their signs that attracted me: "Peace At Any Cost."

The young woman who had the placard was unhappily trying to pound a nail with the heel of her shoe, in an attempt to reconnect her soggy sign to a stake.

"So, how much are you spending?" I asked.

"Whatd'ya mean?" she scowled.

"What's peace costing you?" I questioned.

Her answer about bowled me over. "It's not personal peace I want—it's world peace!"

That's when I started humming a ditty that went something like, "Let there be peace on earth, and let it begin with me."

—PAUL M. MILLER

UNDER HIS WINGS

❧

Under His wings, under His wings,

Who from His love can sever?

Under His wings my soul shall abide,

Safely abide forever.

—WILLIAM O. CUSHING

Peace does not dwell in outward things, but within the soul; we may preserve it in the midst of the bitterest pain, if our will remains firm and submissive. Peace in this life springs from acquiescence to, not in an exemption from, suffering.

—FRANCOIS DE FENELON

Cast Out Fear
Give us peace with Thee
Peace with men
Peace with ourselves,
And free us from all fear.

—DAG HAMMARSKJOLD

Peace is more important than all justice; and
peace was not made for the sake of justice,
but justice for the sake of peace.

—MARTIN LUTHER

Because the Lord is my Shepherd,
I have everything I need!

—PSALM 23:1 TLB

 IS RESTORATION

He lets me rest in the meadow grass
and leads me beside the quiet streams.
He restores my failing health. He helps me
do what honors him the most.

—PSALM 23:2-3 TLB

 IS FEARLESSNESS

Even when walking through the dark valley of death
I will not be afraid, for you are close beside me.

—PSALM 23:4 TLB

 IS BLESSING

You have welcomed me as your guest;
blessings overflow!

—PSALM 23:5 TLB

 IS ETERNAL

Your goodness and unfailing kindness shall
be with me all of my life, and afterwards
I will live with you forever.

—PSALM 23:6 TLB

A BENEDICTION

May the God of peace,
    who through the blood of the eternal
covenant brought back from the dead our Lord
Jesus, that great Shepherd of the sheep, equip
you with everything good for doing his will,
and may he work in us what is pleasing to him,
through Jesus Christ, to whom be glory for ever
and ever. Amen.

—HEBREWS 13:20-21

Additional copies of this book
are available from your local bookstore.

OTHER TITLES FROM HONOR BOOKS:

The Fruit of the Spirit Is Love • The Fruit of the Spirit Is Joy • The Fruit of the Spirit Is Kindness

If you have enjoyed this book, or if it has
impacted your life, we would like to hear from you.
Please contact us at:

Department E • P.O. Box 55388 • Tulsa, Oklahoma 74155

HONOR BOOKS
Tulsa, Oklahoma